RIOT SURVIVAL

RIOT SURVIVAL

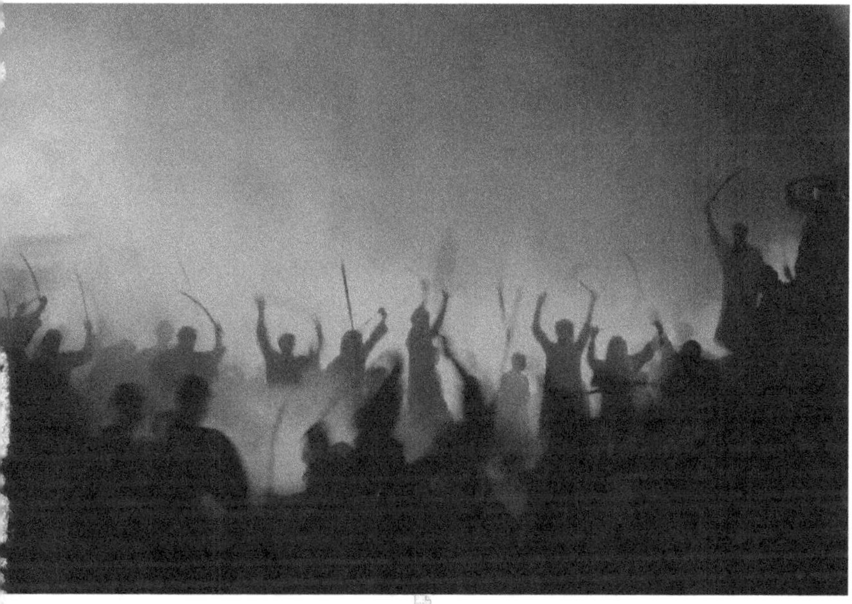

David Holman

RIOT SURVIVAL

Preparation

David Holman

SURVIVALIST INC

RIOT SURVIVAL

TABLE OF CONTENTS

Riot Control Agents 8

Riot Survival Kit 9

LEGAL DISCLAIMER

THE INFORMATION CONTAINED IN RIOT SURVIVAL IS MEANT TO SERVE AS A COMPREHENSIVE COLLECTION OF TIME-TESTED AND PROVEN STRATEGIES THAT THE AUTHORS OF THIS COURSE LEARN OVER THE YEARS, RELATED TO EMERGENCY PREPAREDNESS.

THE MATERIAL IN RIOT SURVIVAL MAY INCLUDE INFORMATION, PRODUCTS, OR SERVICES BY THIRD PARTIES. THIRD PARTY MATERIALS COMPRISE OF THE PRODUCTS AND OPINIONS EXPRESSED BY THEIR OWNERS. AS SUCH, THE AUTHORS OF THIS GUIDE DO NOT ASSUME RESPONSIBILITY OR LIABILITY FOR ANY THIRD PARTY MATERIAL OR OPINIONS. THE PUBLICATION OF SUCH THIRD PARTY MATERIALS DOES NOT CONSTITUTE THE AUTHORS' GUARANTEE OF ANY INFORMATION, INSTRUCTION, OPINION, PRODUCTS OR SERVICE CONTAINED WITHIN THE THIRD PARTY MATERIAL.

WHETHER BECAUSE OF THE GENERAL EVOLUTION OF THE INTERNET, OR THE UNFORESEEN CHANGES IN COMPANY POLICY AND EDITORIAL SUBMISSION GUIDELINES, WHAT IS STATED AS FACT AT THE TIME OF THIS WRITING, MAY BECOME OUTDATED OR SIMPLY INAPPLICABLE AT A LATER DATE. THIS MAY APPLY TO THE MOBS RIOTS AND LOOTERS AS WELL AS THE VARIOUS SIMILAR COMPANIES THAT WEHAVE REFERENCED IN THIS EBOOK, AND OUR SEVERAL COMPLEMENTARY GUIDES. GREAT EFFORT HAS BEEN EXERTED TO SAFEGUARD THE ACCURACY OF THIS WRITING. OPINIONS REGARDING SIMILAR WEBSITE PLATFORMS HAVE BEEN FORMULATED AS A RESULT OF BOTH PERSONAL EXPERIENCE, AS WELL AS THE WELL DOCUMENTED EXPERIENCES OF OTHERS.

A riot is deined as civil unrest characterized by intense bursts of violence.

History has proven that deadly riots can occur for the simplest and mundane reasons. Soccer games have incited violence many times in the past. Only a couple of years ago, a riot broke out in Vancouver after a championship hockey game. If riots can start over such small things, the violence and disorder that would occur after a large scale event such as economic collapse or a terrorist attack would be devastating.

Riots are dangerous and deadly. An estimated one million people died during the civil unrest that followed India's independence. Thousands of people die each year from rioting and related violence. Although angry outbursts can sometimes be anticipated, many times riots break out without warning. The confusion and destruction associated with a terrorist attack could force entire cities of people to riot out of fear and uncertainty.

Preparation

Preparing ahead of time for any type of disaster scenario is always a good idea. After a natural disaster or attack, you will not be able to rely on emergency services or law enforcement. These services will be overwhelmed and unavailable for many emergency situations.

A key component of successful survival in any situation is planning. Whether a natural disaster wipes out an area, a terrorist attack kills millions, or an EMP leaves the electrical grid in shambles, having a survival plan could mean the difference between life and death. When a catastrophic event occurs, the supply chain will be interrupted. This means no food on store shelves, no medicine at the pharmacy, and no help from government agencies for weeks or even longer.

NO
JUSTICE
NO PEACE

The best way to survive the rioting and violence that will ensue after such an attack is to avoid the affected area at all costs. Having a well-conceived plan ahead of time means you will not be forced into action immediately following a disaster. One of the safest places to be during a riot is inside. The ability to stay safely within the conines of your home (if possible and safe to do so) is an extremely valuable asset during a crisis. This means having at least a 10 to 14 day supply of food, required medications, adequate clothing, and even weapons to defend yourself if the rioters get too close.

Obviously if the riot is too close or if your home has been damaged during the disaster, staying where you are is not the ideal scenario. Leaving your home during a riot is dangerous. Leaving your home during a riot without irst having a plan for escape

can be deadly. If you are forced to leave your home and seek shelter elsewhere, it is mperative to have an escape plan. Many of the normal routes you might take to leave could be blocked, damaged, or full of violent rioters. Understanding all possible escape routes before a disaster strikes allows you to rationally assess each potential roadway and circumvent those that present an unacceptable amount of danger.

Remember that riots can and will break out for seemingly inconsequential reasons. Even during these outbursts, people often die or suffer serious injuries. The level of violence during a post- disaster riot will be exponentially more severe and the area should be avoided at all costs. Part of what makes riots so dangerous, however, is the sheer unpredictability of them. A peaceful crowd one minute can turn grotesquely violent the next with little to no external provocation. This means that no matter how well you have prepared beforehand, all your planning could go up in smoke at a moment's notice and you may find yourself right n the middle of a full-scale, deadly riot.

When Planning Isn't Enough

Any survivalist expert will agree that planning typically has the greatest impact on your chances of survival during and immediately following a catastrophic event. Those same experts also agree that no matter how much planning you do, it may not be enough. No one really knows just how severe the impact of a natural disaster or terrorist attack will be or how it will affect the population of the area. For this reason, it is important to understand how to maximize your chances of survival if you cannot safely escape the area and wind up in the midst of the chaos.

Remain Calm

A skill often taught to soldiers is how to remain calm under intense pressure.

The techniques for accomplishing this vary to some extent but the idea is that remaining calm allows for rational thought processes. If you panic, irrational thoughts and actions will take hold and you will usually find yourself in a more precarious position.

Deep breathing exercises are a quick way to keep your emotions in check. Take about two minutes to focus on nothing other than your breathing. This calms you down and lets your brain regain its logical thinking capacity again despite the peril you face.

Armed with a calm demeanor, it becomes much easier to devise an escape plan that minimizes risk.

Be Inconspicuous

The longer you are exposed to the conditions present in a riot the greater your chance for injury becomes. Therefore, your primary objective is to escape the area without drawing unnecessary attention to yourself.

This can be accomplished in a number of ways. Clothing is one of the most obvious. For safety, it is best to wear clothing that covers as much skin as possible. Long sleeved shirts and pants are ideal because the material will protect you from some riot control chemicals that may be employed during the crisis. Do not wear anything that looks like a uniform as rioters may confuse you with law enforcement and try to attack. Try not to wear dark clothing or hooded sweatshirts as these could make you look like a rioter to law enforcement.

Without participating in violence, play the part of a rioter when possible. If crowds of people are chanting, chant with them. You are much less likely to be attacked by the crowd if you appear to be one of them. Avoid making eye contact whenever possible. During a situation like this, many rational people can be extremely aggressive and even just looking at them may invoke a confrontation. Move with your head down at a reasonable pace. Running or walking too quickly will draw attention to your intent of leaving the area.

Move With the Crowd

Think of a riotous mob like a strong river current. It is impossible for an average person to swim upstream against a strong river current. You will succumb to exhaustion quickly and could even drown. Moving against an aggressive crowd is just as hazardous. Moving in the opposite direction of rioters not only makes it obvious that you are not one of them but it also increases the chances of a confrontation as you fight against crowds of people.

The best way to move toward an exit when stuck in the middle of a crowd is to move in the direction of the crowd while slowing moving toward the outside. Traveling directly toward the outer limits of the crowd looks suspicious. If you move slowly toward the outside, it is likely that people will not notice. Once you have gotten outside the center of the violence it is easier to determine the best escape route and get there inconspicuously.

The one exception to this rule is if you notice the crowd moving into a bottleneck. This might be a tunnel, fenced area, or high walled enclosure that forces the crowd into a tight place. Often confined rioters will become even more volatile and violent. If the crowd is moving dangerously close to a bottleneck, it is better to risk looking suspicious and get to the side and away from that area as quickly as possible.

Getting Inside

Whenever possible, get indoors quickly. Typically the worst violence during a riot occurs out in the streets where the majority of people are concentrated. Buildings can

offer safety for those looking to escape the riot and not participate. Keep in mind that if rioters notice you entering a building they may also enter and this can leave you trapped and vulnerable.

For this reason, it is best to get away from the larger concentrations of people before attempting to enter a building. People on the outskirts of an angry mob are typically less violent than those right in the middle. These slightly calmer individuals will be less likely to display hostility towards you for attempting to seek shelter.

Make sure that if you do decide to enter a building it is not a private residence. You can easily be shot by a homeowner that mistakes you for a rioter if you barge into their home unannounced.

Large, public access facilities are usually the best buildings to look for although government buildings and financial institutions are often targeted during a riot. These types of buildings should be avoided if possible due to the likelihood that they will be attacked. Even worse, rioters may mistake you for an employee of the institution leaving you more vulnerable to attack.

Driving to Safety

A car provides a quick way to get to safety in many instances. However, the element of blending in with the crowd is gone if you decide to drive. If you live in a suburban area and can escape without traveling through the dense populations of the city, you have the best chances for escaping the area unharmed. If you live in a high population area or are forced to travel through it on your way to safety, a vehicle can present a unique set of challenges.

If the roads are packed with rioters, it will be difficult to navigate through the crowds safely. Many people will be threatened by your vehicle and may try to damage it or even take it for themselves. If you find yourself in a heavily crowded and aggressive area, do not stop the car. Continue driving at a moderate pace and use your horn to let people know you are coming through. If you move too fast, rioters or law enforcement may see you as a threat. Moving too slowly makes your vehicle an easy target for attack.

Often people who attempt to flee the area in a vehicle do not make it as far as they intend. The roads may be closed due to damage or a police barricade. Rioters may attack the vehicle forcing them to abandon it and move to safety. Be prepared to ditch the car. Police are often instructed not to let anyone past the barricade during a riot. Moving on foot may afford you an alternative route around the barricade. In truly desperate times following a disaster, your vehicle may look like the perfect escape vehicle for others.

Protecting your car is not worth your life. If aggressive rioters

attempt to seize your vehicle, it is usually best to let them have it and move discreetly to safety along the perimeter of the violence.

If you are fortunate to get outside of the affected area continue driving for as long as it

:akes to get to a safe location. This may be a relative's house in a neighboring city or another

oug out location that you have pre-designated during your survival planning. Even when you

feel that you are far enough away from the situation, remember to stay vigilant. Rioters can

quickly spread from the violent epicenter and could be moving toward your location.

Riot Control Agents

Law enforcement is usually armed with a variety of riot control tools ranging from chemicals

to rubber bullets. If you know you will be traveling through a riot-stricken area, plan for riot

control techniques to minimize injury to yourself. Long sleeved clothing and pants will keep

chemical agents from contaminating your exposed skin.

Airborne chemical agents such as tear gas or pepper spray can make it almost impossible to navigate your way to safety. Although having a gas mask is the most effective method to prevent falling victim to these agents, wearing a gas mask will make you stand out in a crowd and make you more susceptible to attack. Instead, consider carrying a solution that is half water and half liquid antacid in a spray bottle. Especially effective on pepper spray, the antacid solution will help minimize the effects of the chemical agent.

The same solution can be sprayed on all exposed skin to neutralize the burning effects of these chemical agents. Although exposure to the mucous membranes is usually the most painful, any exposed skin will burn from direct exposure.

Tear gas makes breathing especially dificult. Carrying rags soaked in vinegar, lemon juice, or even water and covering your mouth with them makes breathing after tear gas deployment much easier. The chemical components of the gas will be absorbed by the wet rags.

Avoid touching your face during a chemical agent attack. This can spread the chemicals around and actually make the effects more severe. If you wear corrective contact lenses, be sure to remove them and wear glasses before making an escape attempt. If chemical riot agents get under the contact lens, the effects are compounded making it impossible to see.

Rubber bullets are another tactic used by law enforcement during a riot.

Although designed to be a non-lethal form of ammunition, a direct hit to the head or

another sensitive area of the body could lead to death or serious injury at the very least. Some experts recommend wearing a helmet to protect your head from rubber bullets and debris possibly thrown by the crowd. Although this is an option, wearing a helmet could make you appear like a law enforcement officer to an aggressive crowd subjecting you to a higher risk for attack.

The best defense against rubber bullets or high pressure water is to stay away from them whenever possible. If you move smartly through the crowd while locating an exit, you will often avoid being in a direct line of assault from these devices. If you find yourself in an area where you may get hit, try to be as non-aggressive as possible while you move away from the area. If you look like a passive bystander you are less likely to be targeted by law enforcement personnel.

Riot Survival Kit

Riots can erupt suddenly. A volatile economy responsible for historic unemployment rates, recent terrorist attacks, and a slew of powerful natural disasters mean that a large scale riot could occur at any time. Armed with this knowledge, you should take the time to assemble a simple riot survival kit that can be accessed quickly when a catastrophe happens and violence is inevitable.

1. Clothing - Long sleeve clothing and pants will prevent your skin from being exposed to chemical agents that may be deployed by law enforcement. Make sure the clothing does

not resemble any type of uniform as this may make you more susceptible to attack by rioters.

1. Small amount of cash - After social collapse, you may be required to bribe law enforcement officials to get past a police barricade and leave the affected area. You will also need money to purchase food and other supplies once you have safely evacuated.

2. Small knife - A knife can be used for many purposes in any survival situation. It can also be used as a weapon if escaping from an angry mob becomes impossible.

3. Extra cell phone - Most people have a cell phone already but it is a good idea to purchase a second inexpensive model that can be stored in your riot kit.

4. Battery operated radio - A radio allows you to listen for changes in the situation and can alert you to areas where it is not safe to travel.

5. Flashlight - A flashlight is a necessity in the dark or if you enter a building for safety. The power is likely to be out as a result of the initial disaster which can make moving around very difficult without some form of light.

6. Map of the area - Especially when traveling on foot, a map provides insight about possible alternate routes when primary travel routes become impassable.

7. Matches - Matches stored in a waterproof case or plastic resealable bag can be used to start a fire if needed. A lighter can also be used but is also susceptible to water damage if not kept dry.

8. Pepper spray - If you become cornered by aggressive rioters, pepper spray can afford you enough time to escape.

9. Antacid solution - As discussed previously, combining equal parts of liquid antacid and water in a spray bottle will counteract the effects of some chemical agents commonly used to suppress rioters. Spraying the solution on areas of exposed skin will lessen the burning sensation typically associated with exposure by neutralizing the acidic chemicals within the compound.

10. Bandanas or rags - These pieces of cloth can be soaked in water and placed over your mouth allowing for easier breathing in the presence of airborne chemicals. Be sure to change the cloth often as it will quickly become saturated with chemicals and lose its effectiveness.

This list is not meant to be all-inclusive but the items listed should be included in all riot survival kits at a minimum. If you require medications you should pack at least a 72 hour supply in this kit as well. Any other things you can think of that may be specific to your area can also be included. Just make sure the entire kit fits into a bag that can easily and inconspicuously be carried on your back. The last thing you want is a large bag that draws attention to you and is difficult to manage as you move through an angry crowd.

Just like the events that cause them, a riot is a very unpredictable phenomena that is difficult to plan for. Understanding the events surrounding the crisis and practicing the safety techniques outlined in this guide will put you at a distinct advantage over everyone else. This small advantage may very well be what gets you out of the area quickly and efficiently when a riot occurs.

Title: Safety Measures for Dealing with Mobs and Protestors

Mobs and protestors can present a significant safety risk to individuals and property. It is essential to be aware of potential dangers and take appropriate safety measures to protect yourself and others.

1. Stay informed: Keep updated on current events and any planned protests or gatherings in your area. This will allow you to avoid potential danger spots and plan your route accordingly.

2. Avoid the area: If a protest or mob gathering is taking place, it is best to avoid the area altogether. This is particularly true if the event is known to be violent or if law enforcement is present in riot gear.

3. Use caution when traveling: If you must travel through an area where a protest or mob is present, use caution and avoid any confrontations. Keep your windows rolled up and lock your doors, and do not engage with any protestors or members of the mob.

4. Stay calm: In the event that you are confronted by a mob or protestor, it is important to remain calm and not engage in any confrontations. Do not make any sudden movements or provoke the group.

5. Find a safe place: If you are caught in the middle of a mob or protest, find a safe place to take cover, such as a nearby building or car. Stay indoors until the situation has been resolved.

6. Follow the instructions of law enforcement: If law enforcement is present at the scene, follow their instructions and do not resist arrest.

7. Seek medical attention: If you or someone else is injured during a protest or mob incident, seek medical attention immediately.

t is important to remember that mobs and protests can be unpredictable and dangerous. By staying informed, avoiding the area, using caution when traveling, staying calm, finding a safe place, following the instructions of law enforcement and seeking medical attention if needed, you can help ensure your safety in these potentially dangerous situations.

PHOTO
in care

1. Be aware of your surroundings: Keep an eye out for potential hazards, such as broken glass or debris on the ground, and stay away from any objects that could be used as weapons.

2. Wear protective gear: If you expect to be in a potentially violent or dangerous situation, consider wearing protective gear such as a helmet, goggles, and a face mask.

3. Have a plan: Develop a plan of action in case you are confronted by a mob or protestor. This can include identifying safe exits, knowing the location of emergency shelters, and having emergency contact information readily available.

4. Know your rights: Familiarize yourself with your rights when dealing with law enforcement during a protest or mob situation. This can include the right to remain silent, the right to an attorney, and the right to a fair trial.

5. Document the incident: If you are involved in a protest or mob incident, document it by taking photos or videos if it is safe to do so. This can serve as evidence if legal action is taken against the protesters, the police or both.

6. Use non-lethal self defense: If you feel threatened by a mob or protestor, consider using non-lethal self-defense techniques, such as pepper spray, a stun gun, or a flashlight.

7. Have emergency supplies: Have emergency supplies on hand such as water, food, and first aid kit, in case of getting trapped or stranded during an event.

By following these safety measures, you can better protect yourself and others during a mob or protest situation. However, it's important to keep in mind that these events can be highly volatile and unpredictable, and it is always best to err on the side of caution and avoid them if possible.

Title: Safety Measures for Dealing with Looters

Looters can present a significant safety risk to individuals, businesses, and communities during times of civil unrest or natural disasters. It is essential to be aware of potential dangers and take appropriate safety measures to protect yourself, your property and others.

1. Stay informed: Keep updated on current events and any planned looting or gatherings in your area. This will allow you to take appropriate measures to protect your property and plan your route accordingly.

2. Secure your property: Secure your property by locking doors and windows and installing security cameras or alarm systems. Consider boarding up windows or adding security gates to deter looters.

3. Have a plan: Develop a plan of action in case of looting. This can include identifying safe exits, knowing the location of emergency shelters, and having emergency contact information readily available.

4. Have emergency supplies: Have emergency supplies on hand such as water, food, and first aid kit, in case of getting trapped or stranded during an event.

5. Have a communication plan: Have a communication plan with your family and friends to stay in contact during the event.

6. Be aware of your surroundings: Keep an eye out for potential hazards, such as broken glass or debris on the ground, and stay away from any objects that could be used as weapons.

7. Wear protective gear: If you expect to be in a potentially violent or dangerous situation, consider wearing protective gear such as a helmet, goggles, and a face mask.

8. Follow the instructions of law enforcement: If law enforcement is present, follow their instructions and do not resist arrest.

9. Document the incident: If you are involved in a looting incident, document it by taking photos or videos if it is safe to do so. This can serve as evidence if legal action is taken against the looters.

10. Use non-lethal self defense: If you feel threatened by looters, consider using non-lethal self-defense techniques, such as pepper spray, a stun gun, or a flashlight.

It is important to remember that looting can be unpredictable and dangerous. By staying informed, securing your property, having a plan, having emergency supplies, being aware of your surroundings, wearing protective gear, following the instructions of law enforcement, documenting the incident, and using non-lethal self defense, you can help ensure your safety during these potentially dangerous situations.

1. Have a neighborhood watch: Consider forming a neighborhood watch with your neighbors to keep an eye out for suspicious activity in the area. This can help deter looters and provide a sense of community and support during a difficult time.

2. Arm yourself: If it is legal and safe to do so, consider arming yourself with a firearm for self-defense. However, it's important to remember that firearms should only be used as a last resort and only if you are properly trained and licensed to handle them.

3. Have a safe room: Consider having a designated safe room in your home where you can retreat in case of an emergency. This can include a room with a solid door, a deadbolt, and a phone to call for help.

4. Know your rights: Familiarize yourself with your rights when dealing with law enforcement during a looting situation. This can include the right to protect your property, the right to use reasonable force in self-defense and the right to remain silent.

5. Have insurance: Make sure you have adequate insurance coverage for your property and personal belongings, in case they are damaged or stolen during a looting incident.

6. Be prepared for the aftermath: Be prepared for the aftermath of looting, as it can take a long time for services to be restored and for the community to recover. This can include having extra food, water, and other essentials on hand, as well as a plan for dealing with any damage to your property.

By following these safety measures, you can better protect yourself, your property and others during a looting situation. However, as always, it's important to keep in mind that looting can be highly volatile and unpredictable, and it is always best to err on the side of caution and take proactive measures to prepare for the worst.

Top of Form

Title: Safety Measures for Dealing with Flash Mobs

Flash mobs can present a significant safety risk to individuals and communities, particularly in crowded urban areas. Flash mobs are spontaneous gatherings of people, often organized through social media, that can quickly turn violent or destructive. It is essential to be aware of potential dangers and take appropriate safety measures to protect yourself and others.

1. Stay informed: Keep updated on current events and any planned flash mobs in your area. This will allow you to avoid potential danger spots and plan your route accordingly.

2. Avoid the area: If a flash mob is taking place, it is best to avoid the area altogether. This is particularly true if the event is known to be violent or if law enforcement is present in riot gear.

3. Use caution when traveling: If you must travel through an area where a flash mob is present, use caution and avoid any confrontations. Keep your windows rolled up and lock your doors, and do not engage with any members of the flash mob.

4. Stay calm: In the event that you are confronted by a flash mob, it is important to remain calm and not engage in any confrontations. Do not make any sudden movements or provoke the group.

5. Find a safe place: If you are caught in the middle of a flash mob, find a safe place to take cover, such as a nearby building or car. Stay indoors until the situation has been resolved.

6. Follow the instructions of law enforcement: If law enforcement is present at the scene, follow their instructions and do not resist arrest.

7. Seek medical attention: If you or someone else is injured during a flash mob incident, seek medical attention immediately.

8. Document the incident: If you are involved in a flash mob incident, document it by taking photos or videos if it is safe to do so. This can serve as evidence if legal action is taken against the participants.

It is important to remember that flash mobs can be unpredictable and dangerous. By staying informed, avoiding the area, using caution when traveling, staying calm, finding a safe place, following the instructions of law enforcement and seeking medical attention if needed, and document the incident, you can help ensure your safety in these potentially dangerous situations.

1. Be aware of social media: Keep an eye out for potential flash mob gatherings being organized through social media and stay away from the area if one is planned near you.
2. Have a communication plan: Have a communication plan with your family and friends to stay in contact during the event.
3. Have emergency supplies: Have emergency supplies on hand such as water, food, and first aid kit, in case of getting trapped or stranded during an event.
4. Know your rights: Familiarize yourself with your rights when dealing with law enforcement during a flash mob situation. This can include the right to remain silent, the right to an attorney, and the right to a fair trial.
5. Use non-lethal self defense: If you feel threatened by a flash mob, consider using non-lethal self-defense techniques, such as pepper spray, a stun gun, or a flashlight.
6. Have a plan for your business or property: If you are a business owner, have a plan in place for protecting your property and employees in case of a flash mob. This can include securing doors and windows, installing security cameras, and having a communication plan with employees.
7. Report criminal activities: If you witness criminal activities such as vandalism, theft or physical assault, report it to the police immediately.

By following these safety measures, you can better protect yourself and others during a flash mob situation. However, as always, it's important to keep in mind that flash mobs can be highly volatile and unpredictable, and it is always best to err on the side of caution and take proactive measures to prepare for the worst.

In summary, mobs, protestors, looters and flash mobs can present significant safety risks to individuals and communities. It is essential to stay informed, avoid the area if possible, use caution when traveling, remain calm, find a safe place, follow the instructions of law enforcement, and seek medical attention if needed. Other important safety measures include being aware of your surroundings, wearing protective gear, having a plan, having emergency supplies, documenting the incident, using non-lethal self defense, knowing your rights, having a neighborhood watch, having insurance, being prepared for the aftermath, having a communication plan and arm yourself if legal and safe to do so.

If you find yourself caught in one of these situations, it is important to remain calm and avoid any confrontations. Follow the instructions of law enforcement and seek medical attention if needed. If you are able to do so safely, document the incident with photos or videos. Remember that these events can be highly volatile and unpredictable, and it is always best to err on the side of caution and take appropriate measures to protect yourself and others.

Have a pre-plan: Prepare for the possibility of these events happening by having a pre-plan in place. This can include having emergency contact numbers, knowing the location of emergency shelters, and having a designated meeting place with your family or friends in case of an emergency.

Listen to the authorities: Follow the instructions of the local authorities and comply with any evacuation or lockdown orders.

Know the signs of escalating violence: Be aware of the signs that a peaceful gathering is escalating into a violent one, such as the presence of weapons, confrontational behavior, and increased shouting or chanting.

Don't get trapped: If you find yourself in a mob or a protest, try to avoid getting trapped in a confined area or a dead-end street, as it can make it harder for you to escape.

Be mindful of your body language: Avoid making direct eye contact or aggressive gestures that could be interpreted as a provocation or a challenge. Don't carry valuables: Avoid carrying anything of value, such as jewelry, credit cards, or cash, as they might attract the attention of looters.

Have a first aid kit: Have a first aid kit on hand, as injuries can happen during these situations.

Report any suspicious activity: If you see anything suspicious, such as someone trying to incite violence, report it to the authorities immediately. Be prepared for the aftermath: Be prepared for the aftermath of these events,

as it can take a long time for services to be restored and for the community to recover. This can include having extra food, water, and other essentials on hand, as well as a plan for dealing with any damage to your property.

It's worth noting that these events can be highly chaotic, and it's important to have a plan and be prepared to act on it quickly. The most important thing is to remain calm and make decisions based on your personal safety and the safety of those around you.

David Holman

SurvivalistInc.com